CRAFTSMAN'S GUIDES

PICTURE FRAMING TECHNIQUES

Mark Lister

CHARTWELL
BOOKS, INC

For Jill and Devon

Notes: Throughout this book, American terms are signalled in parentheses after their British equivalents the first time in each section they occur. In frame and artwork measurement, height always precedes width.

Editors: Alison Leach and Anne Yelland
Editorial consultant: Fanny Campbell
Editorial assistant: Catherine Tilley
Art director: Elaine Partington
Art editor: David Allen
Designers: Roger Kohn and Su Martin
Illustrator: Steve Cross
Photography: Jon Bouchier
Studio: Del & Co
Picture research: Liz Eddison

CHARTWELL BOOKS
A division of Book Sales, Inc.
POST OFFICE BOX 7100
114 Northfield Avenue
Edison, N.J. 08818-7100

CLB 4486
© 1995 CLB Publishing, Godalming, Surrey, U.K.
All rights reserved
Printed and bound in Singapore
ISBN 0-7858-0401-3

Contents

Introduction

A home with bare walls can be as cold and sterile in atmosphere as a house with boarded-up windows. Pictures, whether simple family photographs, posters or more valuable subjects such as oils, water-colours or limited edition prints, can make an enormous difference to your rooms. It is not necessary, however, to spend a great deal of money to have them framed: many pictures can be framed well and inexpensively by the amateur.

The framing of a picture does not wholly depend on the artist's interpretation of the work. The choice of frame or mount (mat) will vary according to the room, its decor and to the type of picture. The finished article must harmonize with its surroundings, regardless of the quality and value of the article being framed. It's your home, you must decide. You wouldn't, for example, frame a parking ticket in a gilt surround and place it in the main room of the house. Common sense and taste will dictate which subject goes best in which room.

It does not follow necessarily that either a good oil painting or a costly print should be framed with an expensive surround (frame) and mount; often a plain wooden frame will suffice. Equal care should of course be taken with a simple and inexpensive subject – a page from a calendar, for example – as with more prestigious subjects. There are, however, certain steps that must be taken with more valuable subjects and it is advisable to obtain professional advice before you attempt to frame an irreplaceable work of art.

Picture framing techniques

This book has been set out in projects, each one becoming progressively more involved. Projects 1 and 2 are simple and require very basic tools. They are good starting points. From the experience you gain with these simpler items you should feel confident to attempt the further, more complicated, projects. None of these projects are beyond the scope of the amateur and you will find helpful advice about each one throughout the book.

At the end of the book are ideas for further framing projects and advice on tackling more unusual subjects.

A home must have an atmosphere and part of that atmosphere is created with the decor. Pictures are pleasing and need not be expensive. Many local shops and auctions often have available good quality water-colours and prints, which, when framed, can transform a room.

The secret of a good picture frame is to present the picture as a whole: it is not good enough just to find a frame a picture will fit into in the hope that the quality of the artwork will blind the eye to its presentation. When hung, the complete picture forms the decoration.

Tools

None of the tools used for the projects in this book are specifically designed for picture framing and many have other uses in the home. There are specialist tools on the market, and these may produce a slightly better finished article, but they can be expensive, and will probably be rarely used. Many competent amateur picture framers produce excellent results using only the tools mentioned here.

A sharp craft knife, preferably the type with a 'break-off' blade - these are sharper than non 'break-off' blades.

A bradawl for making holes.

A rule at least 1m (1yd) long; this should be graduated in both metric and Imperial measurements.

A straight-edge, also at least 1m (1yd) long; this should be made of steel and have one bevelled edge.

A pin hammer is more suitable than a claw or ball hammer.

A cylindrical sharpening stone, preferably the type used to sharpen sickles.

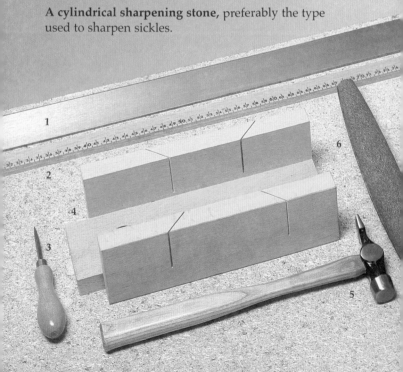

A mitre block to hold the saw blade at exactly 45° when sawing.

A fine-toothed saw with as many teeth per centimetre or inch as possible.

A modeller's drill is used for drilling holes in moulding. This is a small hand-held electric drill, specially designed for working on small articles.

A 150mm (6in.) vice (vise) has a larger jaw area than an engineer's vice and holds the piece of timber firmly but with less risk of damage.

A staple gun is preferable to a sturdy desk-top stapler, although you could open one of these up and use it.

A pair of pliers

1 Straight-edge; 2 rule; 3 bradawl; 4 mitre block; 5 pin hammer; 6 sharpening stone; 7 staple gun; 8 craft knife; 9 craft knife with break-off blade; 10 fine-toothed saw; 11 pliers; 12 modeller's drill; 13 vice.

Materials

Frame mouldings, mount cards (mat cardboards) and some specialized fittings must be obtained from an artists' materials shop.

All the other materials mentioned in this book are in general everyday use, and can be obtained from DIY (hardware) stores, timber merchants, picture framers, and good stationers. Because of the vast range of frame mouldings, mount cards and fittings it is not practicable to categorize them all in a book of this size: the specific requirements are explained in each project. In general, high-quality materials are expensive.

Mounts

The mount is a card surround (cardboard frame), sometimes known as the mat, and comes in thicknesses ranging from nos. 1-12 sheet and in various colours. Thickness no. 1 is approximately the same as that used for a packet of breakfast cereal (thickness no. 12 is twelve times as thick).

Glass

Throughout the book, we have assumed that you would not wish to store glass at home. It is easier for the amateur to go to a glazier and obtain glass cut to size. Three types of glass are used in picture framing:

2mm (¹⁄₁₂in.) sheet glass is produced by rolling to the required thickness. This is often imperfect, but cheap; the imperfection can give a good effect with old prints.

2mm (¹⁄₁₂in.) float glass is produced by modern methods and is perfectly flat.

2.5mm (¹⁄₁₀in.) non-reflecting glass is semi-opaque and is used to reduce the reflections from the picture, but it can obscure fine detail and produce a hazy effect. It is often used with modern posters.

Right: *There are thousands of different mouldings and hundreds of different mount cards and colours. The skill of the framer is to select from this vast assortment the frame and mount best suited to each particular picture.*

Project 1: Family photograph

Clip framing

Clip framing on hardboard (masonite) is one of the simpler ways to frame a picture. It's quick and easy, and ideal for basic subjects such as photographs, certificates and even some small pictures which might be over-powered by a larger frame. The maximum safe size of subject for this method of display is about 500 × 400mm (20 × 16in.). This is because the weight of the glass is held by clips, and each clip causes a pressure point on the glass. The larger the glass, the more pressure is put on it by the clips; too much pressure can cause the glass to shatter. Larger subjects should be covered by Perspex (plexiglas) rather than by glass; however, this is liable to be scratched more easily and also attracts static.

This project is an ideal introduction to picture framing, since many of the techniques involved are fundamental to the craft. The subject must first be trimmed to size, then measured and the glass obtained. The glass is then used as a template for measuring and cutting the hardboard backing for the subject. Hangers are fixed to the backing and the whole is then ready for assembly.

Mounts (mats) are often not used with this type of frame, and will not be cut here. This is because the thickness of material which the clips will hold is limited; a mount, in addition to the subject, glass and hardboard can make the whole assembly too thick for the clips.

French and Swiss clips

Two different types of securing clips can be used for this type of framing – French spring clips, and Swiss clips. French clips are easier to fix, and are satisfactory for most subjects. Swiss clips (sometimes called Emo clips) produce a more attractive result, since less of the metal clip is visible on the front of the picture. They are more difficult to fix, however, and care is needed to avoid breaking the glass. Here, French clips will be used.

The tools needed to complete this project will probably be found around the home (see pp. 8-9). The necessary materials can be obtained from a glazier, timber merchant, DIY (hardware) store and artists' supplier.

Left: *Clip framing is relatively inexpensive and ideal for family and school photographs. These frames are simple to construct and transform nooks and crannies around the house.*

Trimming

Many photographs are printed with a white border around them. If your photograph has a surrounding border, this will probably need trimming to ensure that the whole is kept in perspective. It is usual for the borders at both the top and the sides of a picture to be of equal measurements, and for the one at the bottom to be slightly deeper. This is to avoid the optical illusion of the picture falling out of the frame.

Use a sharp craft knife and the straight-edge to cut the edges to size. Scissors will not produce a straight cut and any inaccuracies at this stage will affect the finished result.

Measuring

Decide which type of glass you wish to use (see p. 10). To determine the size of glass to buy, measure the picture to its full trimmed size and subtract 3mm (⅛in.) to allow for inaccuracies by the glazier. It is far easier to trim the card or paper borders of the picture than it is to trim the glass afterwards.

It is necessary to buy the glass before you can proceed with the project, since subsequent measurements are all based on the size of the glass.

Method of assembly

Place the piece of glass on the picture, match them up, and pencil around the edges of the glass on to the picture, then trim along the pencilled lines using a straight-edge and a sharp craft knife. If your trimming is accurate, the picture and the glass should now both be exactly the same size.

Place the glass on a piece of 3.2mm (⅛in.) hardboard, matching one corner of the glass with one corner of the board. Using the pencil, mark out the size of the glass on to the board, then cut the hardboard with the straight-edge and the craft knife. Aim to cut about 0.5mm (¹⁄₃₂in.) inside the pencilled marks, then smooth off the edges of the board with sandpaper.

Place the hardboard on the work surface, with the glass on top and check that they are identical in size.

The next step is to attach the 'D' rings to hold the hanging cord to the back of the hardboard, so you must now decide which way you would like the photograph to hang.

Measuring and trimming

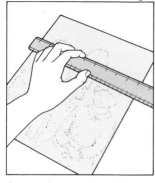

1 *Buy glass to trimmed image size.*

2 *Use glass as a template for final trimming.*

3 *Trim picture to exact glass size.*

4 *Cut backing hardboard to exact glass size.*

5 *Smooth edges of hardboard with sandpaper.*

6 *Backing, image and glass should all be the same size.*

'D' rings

'D' rings are either of single- or double-hole format; the latter are used for pictures measuring more than 500×500mm (20×20in.). It is usual to fix them to the hardboard with bifurcated or splittable rivets. To avoid any irregularities from the hardboard, such as the little bumps from the rivets showing through to the picture, a thin lining or intermediary backing should be used between the hardboard and the back of the picture. The thickness of cardboard used to package breakfast cereals is ideal.

The 'D' rings should be placed about one-third of the way down the back of the hardboard and about one-sixth of the board's width from the edges. For small pictures it is only necessary to use one 'D' ring, placed centrally near the top of the hardboard. Make holes for the rings slightly smaller in diameter than the size of the rivets, using the bradawl and working from the smooth side to the rough. Sand off the side of the holes where the bradawl has emerged on the rough side, then place the rivet through the hole in the ring and the hole in the hardboard. Turn over the hardboard, place it on a firm surface, and splay out the rivet shanks with the bradawl, then tap each of the arms flat using the pin hammer.

Secure hangers and a strong cord are an essential part of a good picture frame.

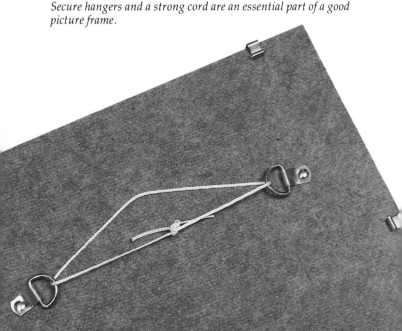

Attaching hangers

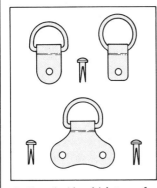

1 First decide which type of hanger to use.

2 Measure location for hangers on hardboard.

3 Make holes for rivets with a bradawl.

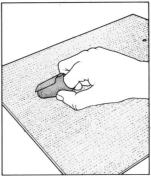

4 Smooth exit hole of bradawl with sandpaper.

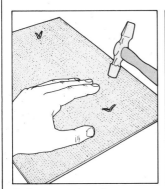

5 Open out rivet; hammer flat with pin hammer.

6 Place card over rivets to prevent marking photograph.

Assembling the picture

Smooth the rough edges off the cut glass using a sharpening stone with a few light strokes *in one direction only*. Clean the glass thoroughly. Any household window cleaning product is adequate, although a 50/50 solution of methylated spirit (wood alcohol) and water is the most effective. Dry the glass and polish off all the residual smears, then brush off any dust with a natural hair soft brush.

Place the hardboard on the work surface with the lining cardboard on top, then the photograph and the glass, all lined up flush with each other. Position one side slightly over the edge of the work surface and open the French spring clips using the two opening arms (these operate in the same way as bulldog clips do). Sandwich

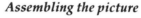

Assembling the picture

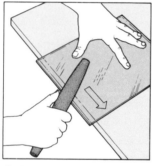

1 *Carefully smooth off edges of glass.*

2 *Clean glass thoroughly with 50/50 meths/water.*

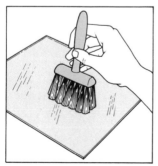

3 *Brush away any dust particles.*

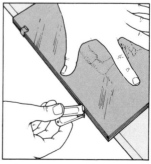

4 *Use French clips to hold assembly together.*

the whole assembly together with the clips, spacing them about 100mm (4in.) apart, all around the picture. Finally tie a piece of nylon cord to the two 'D' rings doubling up on the knots (see pp. 74-5). The picture is now ready to hang upon the wall.

Swiss clips

The procedure for assembly with Swiss clips is exactly the same as with French clips, but the edges of the hardboard will need chamfering with a plane. Place the hardboard on a bench or worktop and lightly skim the edges with the plane to create a bevelled edge. This is to ensure the clips fit firmly. The picture must be assembled upside-down, so check that everything is correctly aligned before fitting the clips.

Cover the worktop with a piece of short-pile carpet. With the picture slightly overhanging the edge of the worktop, fix the clips, spacing them as for French clips. Each clip must be lightly tapped with a hammer to embed it into the hardboard: take great care not to break the glass nor to push the clip through the hardboard. It is usually easier to make a starter hole with a bradawl; this presents no problem if you are using 3.2mm (⅛in.) hardboard.

Although untidy from the rear, Swiss clips (**right**) *provide a neater finish from the front.*

Project 2: Poster

Aluminium framing

Aluminium frames are more expensive than ordinary wooden frames but are often more convenient to use as they can be obtained ready cut and there is no wastage. Due to their construction, it is only possible to frame items up to 10mm (⅜in.) in thickness. They are, however, ideal for framing posters.

Aluminium frames are available either ready cut, or they can be cut to size in specialist shops. This avoids the problem of cutting 45° corner angles in the aluminium, which can be tricky without specialist tools. These frames are extremely robust and do not dent easily. They are very easily assembled and just as easy to take apart again should you wish to substitute a different subject of the same size. Aluminium frames are smart in appearance and are widely used in shop displays (they are sometimes referred to as display frames), modern flats and houses, and airport lounges to complement and update decor. They are also now available in a large number of different colours, including a gun metal finish and a brass coloured finish, both of which can be and are used in more traditional surroundings.

Mounting posters

Since most posters are not printed on very heavy paper, they almost always have to be mounted on to card (cardboard) before framing. For the average poster, wet mounting is satisfactory, and this is what will be described here. If, however, you had a valuable poster (or were unsure about the quality and fastness of the ink used), it would be a good idea to take it to a professional picture framer for dry mounting. This is a heat process, which has the same result as wet mounting but does not involve making the poster wet. Thin tissue paper, coated on both sides with heat-activated adhesive, is sandwiched between the poster and the card, and the whole is placed in a hot press for a specified period of time.

All the materials necessary to complete this project can be obtained from a timber merchant, glazier, DIY (hardware) store, and an artists' supplier or professional picture framer's shop.

Posters can be very impressive works of modern art, and fill a whole wall space by themselves. They should be presented flat with a good-quality frame – mounting is not usually necessary.

Preparing the poster

If your poster is printed on a thick piece of card or on thick paper, it would be acceptable to frame it as it is. Most posters, however, are printed on thin paper and to make the presentation a success, it is necessary to mount the poster on to card. Sheet card is manufactured in various colours, and thicknesses ranging from nos. 1-12. No. 1 thickness is approximately as thick as the packaging on breakfast cereals; no. 12 thickness is twelve times as thick. Card thickness is also sometimes measured in microns; for example, no. 6 sheet card is 1500 microns, and is ideal for this project.

Wet mounting

Wallpaper paste is used to mount the poster on to the backing card. This smooths out any wrinkles, creases and fold marks in the poster exactly as it does for wallpaper. Apply a little extra paste to any damaged parts and use a felt-tip pen to touch up the colour. Aerosol spray adhesive is often used for heavier papers and photographic paper, but it is not ideal for the typical poster paper as this tends to lift in some parts. Cut the no. 6 sheet card approximately 150mm (6in.) wider all round than the poster. Then, take a piece of brown wrapping paper the same size as the card and apply a thin solution of wallpaper paste suitable for lightweight wallpaper to the paper. This is because once the poster has been pasted and has dried on the card, the card will bend. By pasting the brown paper on the reverse side the bending effect will be counteracted. Allow it to stand for about 10 minutes because while the paste is still wet, the paper will expand. Remove the excess adhesive with a paintbrush, then place the bottom edge of the paper down on to the card. Attach the paper exactly as if you were wallpapering, smoothing out the air bubbles with a soft cloth. Turn the card over and leave to dry for 10 minutes. Repeat this process with the poster, again allowing it to stand for about 10 minutes. It is important not to rush this part of the job. Be very careful when you smooth out the poster not to put too great a pressure on to the poster surface. Some posters are poorly printed and it is possible that you might remove some of the ink.

Cover the poster with a piece of old sheet and put it under a few heavy books to keep it flat. Leave it until dry; this usually takes approximately two hours.

Wet mounting

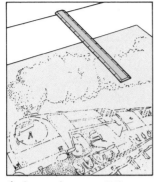

1 Cut card approx. 150mm (6 in.) larger than poster.

2 Paste brown paper to rear of card.

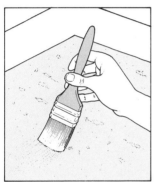

3 Paste poster. Remove excess glue with brush.

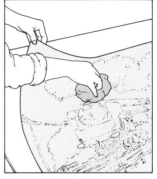

4 Smooth poster flat with a duster.

5 Place under cloth with heavy books on top.

6 Touch in defects with a felt-tipped pen.

Measuring

When the poster is dry, take its measurements. On most posters it is possible to deduct 3mm (1/8in.) from the actual size to allow for inaccuracies by the glazier (see p. 14). If, however, the layout of your poster does not allow you to do this - it may, for example, have lettering, or a signature, or an integral part of the artwork too near the edge - you will have to take the actual measurements and buy the glass to this size.

If you can, buy your frame from a supplier who will cut the aluminium to the exact glass size you require. Ready-cut kits are available (usually in multiples of 50mm/2in.) and in an increasingly wide selection of styles. Once you know the size you need, you may find a kit to fit exactly. If not, then have the frame cut to size. A local picture framing shop should be able to fulfil either or both of these options.

Although relatively new on the market, there are now hundreds of aluminium frames to choose from.

Preparation for assembly

Lay the glass on the poster, making sure that the subject is central, and pencil around the edges of the glass. Then, trim along the pencilled lines using a straight-edge and a craft knife: make sure that the knife is razor sharp or it may cause a tear in the poster. The poster and the glass should now be exactly the same size.

Place the glass on the hardboard (masonite), matching up one of the corners. Mark out the size of the glass on the hardboard with a pencil and cut it, using the straight-edge and craft knife. Cut the hardboard about 0.5mm (1/32in.) inside the pencilled marks, then smooth off the edges of the board with sandpaper.

If you have bought a ready-cut frame, it is advisable to lay the frame over the poster to ascertain the best way of cutting the poster to size. Again, use the straight-edge and a sharp craft knife to trim the poster.

Assembling the frame

Assemble three sides of the frame. Certain types of hanger have to be fixed to the picture frame before the frame itself is assembled. Check that the hanger can be inserted in the rebate (rabbet) before joining the fourth side. Clean the glass using either a household window-cleaner or (preferably) a 50/50 solution of methylated spirit (wood alcohol) and water.

Insert the glass into the unfinished frame and brush out all the dust with a natural hair soft brush. Slide in the poster over the glass, taking great care not to damage it on the edges of the glass. Place the piece of hardboard on the back of the poster, constantly checking for dust

Assembling aluminium frames

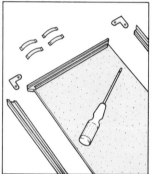

1 Aluminium frames simply 'bolt' together.

2 Assemble three sides, then insert poster.

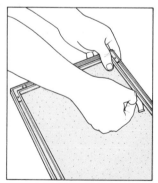

3 Artwork is held in place with springs.

4 Screw banjo hangers to the sides of the frame.

particles; if necessary, you will have to disassemble and brush them away before you fix the final side to the frame. Dust is a particular problem with the large expanses of colour in posters.

Insert the springs at the back of the frame under the rebate. These will ensure that the contents of the frame are pushed flush against the glass. Do not completely push home the springs as they are difficult to remove, should this be necessary. Finally, if you have not already done so, fix the hangers on to the sides of the back of the picture, approximately one-third of the way down the frame, and knot nylon cord to the hangers (see pp. 74-5).

Banjo hangers

Some types of hangers have banjo-shaped holes; these can be fixed at the top of the frame to hang from screws placed in the wall. This enables the picture to hang flush with the wall. They can also be used on the sides of pictures to be hung with nylon cord. Check what is applicable when you buy your frame kit.

Aluminium frame kits contain everything you need to produce an attractive presentation – mouldings, corner plates, clips and hangers.

Project 3: Water-colour

Introduction

Water-colours can be more valuable than either posters or photographs and, for this reason, they are usually displayed in the better rooms of the house. The quality of the painting is often relatively unimportant; many paintings are treasured as much for their sentimental value as for the skill of the artist, and a good choice of frame and mount (mat) can greatly enhance even the most mundane or poorly painted subject.

It is important not only to choose the most appropriate frame and mount for the picture, but also to think about the general decor of the room where the finished subject is to hang. It would look odd, for example, if a Victorian water-colour were framed in a shiny silver aluminium frame and hung in a room furnished with antiques. Look at other water-colours, especially those in museums or historic houses, to build up a mental picture of what goes well with what.

If framing a particularly valuable water-colour, take the special precautions described on p. 73.

Techniques

Although some photographs and posters benefit from a window mount, for the first two projects a mount was not cut. For this water-colour, however, it will be necessary to cut a window mount, and the techniques will be detailed. This is not difficult, but care is needed in order to be successful. It is also possible to decorate a mount with either lines, or a wash, or tapes, or a combination of these three (see pp. 66-7).

As we have seen (pp. 24-5), there is an increasingly wide range of ready-cut picture frame kits on the market, and for some presentations these offer an excellent choice. Cutting your own frame pieces, however, is not difficult, and can be done using a basic mitre block and saw, as long as the pieces are not too wide. This gives a far greater choice of frames.

Gluing and nailing is the best method of joining the pieces for this sort of frame, which has to support the weight of glass and mount card, as well as the artwork and backing. Finally, the painting has to be attached to the mount and the whole assembled.

Left: *The choice of frame and mount card must suit the picture, and complement its surroundings.*

Measuring for a mount

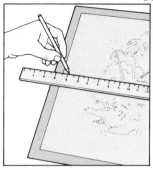
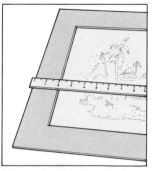

1 Decide border and image size.

2 Twice border size plus image size gives mount size.

Measuring the painting

Although there are no hard and fast rules about the size of a mount around a water-colour, it is usual with an average-sized picture – about 400 × 500mm (16 × 20in.) – to allow a border of 50mm (2in.) at the top and the sides, and about 56mm (2¼in.) at the bottom. The deeper mount at the bottom prevents the optical illusion of the picture falling out of its frame, which can occur when the borders are all equal in width.

Generally, the larger the picture, the larger the mount. However, if the subject is very small, such as a miniature, it is common practice to surround it with a border as wide as 165mm (6½in.). The image size of the water-colour illustrated, or the size of the picture intended to be displayed within the mount, is 360 × 500mm (14¼ × 20in.). Adding 100mm (4in.) to the horizontal measurement of the image size and 106mm (4¼in.) to the vertical measurement for the borders will give us an overall finished framed size of 466 × 600mm (18½ × 24in.). A piece of mount card, therefore, should be cut to these measurements.

The mount

The purpose of a mount is to display the picture in its best possible form. The colour, design and width of a mount are largely a matter of choice, but bear in mind that the mount should enhance a piece of art, not overpower it.

Mount cards were originally manufactured in double

Imperial size 1120 × 800mm (45 × 32in.). Many shops now sell half this size of sheet, known as Imperial size. It is, however, more economical to buy mount card in double Imperial size, so unless you are sure you will only need a small sheet, buy the larger size. (In the USA, mat boards are made in full size 1042 × 800mm/40 × 32in. and in half this size.) For normal picture-framing purposes, a no. 6 sheet mount card (mat cardboard) is adequate as this gives discernible depth between the picture and the surround (frame) and ensures that the surface of the subject is kept clear of the glass. This is not quite so important for a water-colour as, for example, a pastel, where part of the surface of the image could be removed if it stuck to the glass.

The mount should be cut resting on a convenient work surface – a piece of chipboard 13mm (½in.) deep by 1200 × 1200mm (4 × 4ft) is perfectly adequate. Secure the straight-edge, preferably with a nut and bolt, countersinking the head of the bolt into the underneath of the board so that it can be placed on a table without causing any damage. The near side of the straight-edge should overlap the board by about 13mm (½in.). To prevent the board from sliding, place a piece of non-slip material – such as a piece of rubber-backed carpet – between the board and the work top.

Our water-colour's finished size will be 466 × 600mm (18½ × 24in.), so a piece of card must be cut to this size. Firstly, cut off a piece of card approximately 250mm (10in.) wide to use as a cutting strip unless you happen to have an old piece already. Placing this under the mount card and the straight-edge will help to prevent the blade of the knife being blunted on the chipboard; to avoid slipping into a previous cut, shift the cutting strip a little for each cut you make. Next, measure 466mm (18½in.) in from the shorter edge of the mount card, and make pencil marks roughly 150mm (6in.) from the top and from the bottom of the card. Place the card under the straight-edge with both pencil marks just showing on the right and cut just between the straight-edge and the pencil marks. This will ensure that the cut size is just slightly less than the given size, so that the mount card will fit snugly in the frame. Repeat this procedure for the 600mm (24in.) measurement. To check that all the corners are square, measure the two diagonals; these should be the same length. If not, you will have to start again. The defective mount can be used for a smaller painting, provided you make the corners square.

Cutting a window

The window is so called because the four sides left around it themselves create a frame in which the picture sits. It is possible to place the picture on top of the card. This simplifies production, but you do not get the same 'look-in' effect. For this reason, here we will cut out the centre of the card to give the finished subject depth – hence the term window mount. To ensure that the presentation is neat and tidy, bevelled or slant-edged cuts are used. The slant should be approximately 60° to the horizontal. Therefore, the knife must be held at 45-60° to the horizontal to get the correct slanted cut. The technique used is to cross the hands over. Left-handed people must reverse the procedure.

We have already established that the borders are going to be 50mm (2in.) at the top and the sides and 56mm (2¼in.) at the bottom. Measure in from the edges of the card, 50mm (2in.) down from the top edge, 56mm (2¼in.) up from the bottom edge and 50mm (2in.) in from

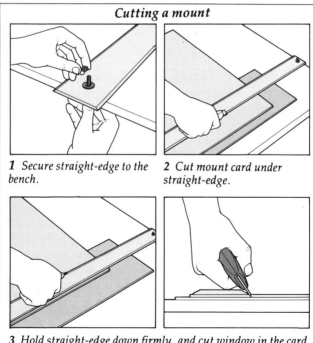

Cutting a mount

1 Secure straight-edge to the bench.

2 Cut mount card under straight-edge.

3 Hold straight-edge down firmly, and cut window in the card, with the knife at a 60° angle.

A carefully chosen window mount with or
without decoration can greatly enhance a watercolour.

the sides, and draw a rectangle joining these measurements on the right side of the card. Place the card under the straight-edge with most of the card showing to the left-hand side. The pencil line should be just visible, about 3mm (⅛in.) from the left-hand side of the straight-edge.

Hold the straight-edge firmly down on the card with your left hand, and cross your right hand over your left to make the cut. Start the cut at the top of the card and work to the bottom. You will only be able to make one clean cut – two or more attempts will not give a good finish – so you must make sure that your knife is as sharp as possible before you begin. It is also important to keep the angle of the knife consistent throughout the cut. As each cut is finished, the mount card should be moved a little on the card underneath it so that the new cut does not fall into a previous cutting groove. It may be necessary to trim the centre corners with a very fine razor blade to make sure that they are square, neat and even. Place the mount over the picture to see that it fits correctly before you proceed.

It is advisable to buy the glass before you join the frame to ensure a perfect fit, so the next step is to purchase the glass. This can then be used as the template for the rest of the framing process. The glass should be ordered to the overall size of the mount.

Cutting a frame

For cutting small frames, a basic mitre block and saw are quite sufficient. To make a reasonable cut on the frame a fine-toothed saw must be used, the more teeth per centimetre or inch the better. A fine-toothed tenon saw or a hacksaw with a 25mm (1in.) deep blade is ideal. The deep blade on the hacksaw prevents the blade twisting in the mitre groove, and producing a ragged cut.

All picture frame measurements are taken from the inside of the rebate (rabbet) to the inside of the opposite rebate. As the rebate is under the frame, it is not possible to see it when cutting. To be able to cut the frame pieces to the correct size, therefore, you must know the overall length of each piece.

The formula for determining this is:

> Glass measurement plus 1.5mm (¹⁄₁₆in.) – for tolerance – plus twice the width of base of frame (that is, without the rebate)
> = overall length of frame piece needed

This gives the length of one frame piece. You need to cut two pieces to this length, then repeat the measuring for the other two pieces (unless you are cutting a square frame). It is a good idea to cut the long lengths first in case you make a mistake; if you do, you can still use these pieces for the short lengths.

Cutting moulding

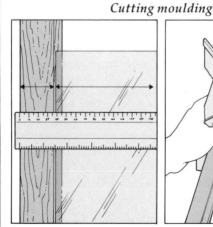

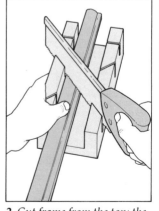

1 *Measure from underneath i.e. including rebate.*

2 *Cut frame from the top; the rebate cannot be seen.*

Common frame types with varying rebates which are easy for the novice to cut using a hand saw and mitre block.

Joining a frame

Although modern contact glues alone are often sufficient for joining frames, the best method of joining a frame is to use both glue and nails. Glue and nails combined have proven themselves over the years, especially for large pictures with thin frames which do not have enough contact area for the glue. You will also need a carpenter's vice (vise) and a small modeller's electric drill; it takes some practice to master this method, but it is inexpensive and widely used.

Firstly, prepare the vice: the back jaw must have a piece of cladding (covering) – plywood is ideal – so that when the frame is placed in the vice, the metal jaw butts up to the rebate and the wooden-covered jaw presses against the back edge of the frame without damaging it. The cladding can be bolted in position. The vice should be attached towards one corner of the workbench and the drill rigged up close by, so that it is handy to reach.

Very small drill bits are difficult to find and tend to break easily, so use a panel pin as a drill bit. For framing small- to medium-sized pictures, thin panel pins approximately 25mm (1in.) long are usually adequate.

To join the frame, take one of the long lengths and place it in the vice with the right-hand end overlapping the vice by 25-38mm (1-1½in.). Next, take one of the short lengths and match up the mitres (45° angles) precisely. It makes it easier to handle the whole assembly if you hold the mitres together with one hand and support the other end of the short length on a small wooden block; this leaves your other hand free for gluing, pinning and drilling. Drill two holes into the join, one near the top and one near the bottom. Larger frames will need three holes. Take care to drill the holes squarely, otherwise the nails will come out at the side of the frame; these holes should be approximately three-quarters of the length of panel pins you intend to use. Once you have drilled the holes, remove the short length, and apply some good-quality wood glue (not a fast-setting glue, this would set too quickly) to one end of the longer piece. Place the short length on to the glued longer length and drive the pins in flush with a pin hammer to form the join.

Remove the two joined lengths from the vice and set aside, then repeat the procedure for the other two lengths. The final joins to complete the frame are easier to make if you have various blocks to support the frame so

Joining a frame

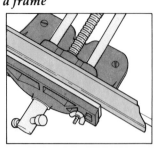

1 Clad the back jaw of the vice to prevent damage to the mouldings, then insert moulding.

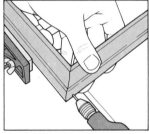

2 Match mitres exactly, and drill two holes.

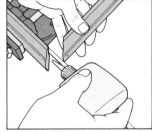

3 Then, apply glue to the joint faces.

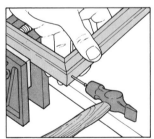

4 Drive home panel pins to secure mitres.

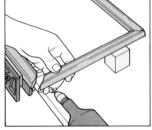

5 Various blocks support the frame as you work.

that the joins are not damaged before the glue is set. When you have finished, set aside the completed frame overnight so that the glue can fully set.

When the frame is dry, touch up the pin heads with the appropriate coloured paint or a felt- or fibre-tipped pen so that they do not show. Alternatively, you could countersink the pins and then fill the holes with nail hole filler, also coloured to match the frame.

Preparing the artwork for assembly

Check the glass and the mount to ensure that they fit into the frame and that both are straight and even.

Many water-colours and prints are executed on thin and often wrinkled paper. These wrinkles must be flattened out before you attach the picture behind the mount to give the picture the best possible presentation. The method used is similar to wet mounting (described on pp. 22-3). Dampen the back of the picture using slightly wet cotton wool and leave it for about 10 minutes. The amount of dampening necessary will depend upon the thickness of the paper; the thicker the paper, the damper it will need to be. Fix a piece of gummed paper tape to the top of the artwork so that the mount can be laid on top. Then, turn the picture over and tape down the three remaining sides of the artwork. When the paper is dry, it will have stretched slightly, and the wrinkles will have disappeared. It is important to assemble the picture before the artwork has completely dried out.

If you have a very valuable subject, do not use the above method, but attach the subject to the mount with two small strips of gummed paper tape to avoid damaging the valuable, and often fragile, paper. When mounting valuable subjects an 'acid-free' board (also known as Conservation/museum board) should be used (see p. 73).

Method of assembly

Lay the glass on a piece of hardboard, pencil round it and cut it out as described on pp. 14-15. Some frames have a narrow rebate, so if you cannot obtain 2mm (1/10in.) hardboard, you may have to chamfer the edges of the hardboard, by trimming along them with a plane.

Place two 'D' rings into the hardboard as described on pp. 16-17, but make sure that the rivets are behind the mount and not behind the artwork. This is because if they were to rust in the future, the rust could go through to the artwork. Alternatively, if your frame is fairly sturdy, attach screw eyes into the sides of the frame.

Clean the glass on both sides, and brush off any dust with a natural hair soft brush. Put the artwork, the mount and the hardboard in place, then turn the whole assembly over, and check for dust. The back can now be fixed to the frame. Hold the hardboard down in place with the side of one hand, leaving your thumb and

Assembling the artwork

1 *Dampen artwork, attach to tape; lay mount over.*

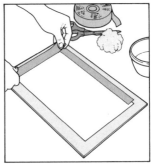

2 *Turn over and tape down three remaining sides.*

3 *Pin the backing into position; rest against block.*

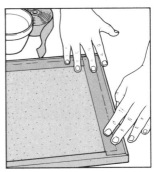

4 *Use tape to seal back and cover gaps.*

forefinger free to hold the panel pins. Tap some of the same type of panel pins you used for joining the frame into the sides of the frame at intervals of about 100mm (4in.) all around the frame.

Now, fix gummed paper tape or masking tape (the former gives a better appearance) over the join between the frame and the hardboard. There are three reasons for doing this: it prevents insects and mites which could damage the painting getting to the artwork; it keeps the frame in place; and it creates a neat appearance.

Finally, fix the nylon hanging cord to the 'D' rings (see pp. 74-5) or on the more robust types of moulding, it would be easier to screw the 'D' rings into the frame rather than rivet the 'D' rings into the hardboard. Alternatively, ordinary screw eyes can be used for small pictures.

Project 4: Oil painting

Stretching and framing a canvas

Oil paintings are usually painted on either canvas or board. Old masters tended to use canvas most of the time, as do professional painters – amateur painters tend to use board. Oils imported from the Far East are invariably painted on canvas, since this is lighter and easier to roll for transportation. Like all canvasses, however, they have to be stretched before framing. This type of oil painting is relatively inexpensive, easily obtainable and very suitable for a first attempt at framing an oil painting.

Oil paintings can be very impressive. They are often larger than many other forms of picture, and it is likely that an oil painting would be displayed in the hall or the living room of the house. The effect of the presentation depends almost entirely on the cost (and, therefore, the quality) of the materials used. An otherwise good oil painting could look dowdy and inferior if just framed with a basic wooden frame, whereas a swept gilt frame would create a presentation worthy of the artist's work – it would also become a feature of the room. You will have to decide what sort of frame is both suitable for the best presentation of the artist's work and would go with the decor and furnishings of your room. Here, however, we will use a fairly traditional frame.

Left and above: *Frame mouldings for oil paintings are expensive and anything other than good quality detracts from the artwork. Choose a frame which complements the canvas.*

Stretching a canvas

If the oil painting is on canvas, you will have to stretch the canvas first (paintings on board do not need stretching).

Canvasses are stretched on stretcher pieces – slotted pieces of wood which all fit together. These are made in multiples of 50mm (2in.), for example 250 × 350mm (10 × 14in.), 300 × 450mm (12 × 18in.) and so on, and come complete with wedges which fit into the internal corners of the frame. (In the USA, these are made in multiples of 25mm/1in. or 50mm/2in. depending on size; the larger stretcher pieces are in multiples of 50mm/2in.) When tapped home, the wedges expand the frame outwards. Buy the stretcher pieces slightly smaller than the image size of the painting on the canvas so that any plain canvas border is not seen after framing. Unfortunately it may be necessary to lose a small piece of the painting.

If your painting does not fit a standard stretcher, it is possible to build up the size of the stretcher by nailing a piece of batten on to the outside of one of the stretcher pieces.

The image size of the painting illustrated, for example, measures 513 × 400 mm (20½ × 16 in.), so it will be necessary to buy stretcher pieces of 400 × 500mm (16 × 20in.) and a piece of batten 13mm (½in.) square and 400mm (16in.) long. Tack (nail) the batten to one of the 400mm (16in.) stretcher pieces so that the 500mm (20in.) piece now measures 513mm (20½in.). Slot the pieces of the stretcher together and square them up. Measure the diagonals to ensure that they are equal – the frame will then be square.

Place the canvas face up on top of the stretcher frame and, starting from the centre top, staple the canvas to the side of the frame using a staple gun. Pull it taut across the frame and staple it to the centre bottom, then pull the canvas to each corner and staple it there. The whole canvas should now be flat. If you are satisfied that it is flat and square, staple it all the way around the stretcher. Stretch it as tight as possible before you insert each staple and keep checking that the stretcher frame is indeed still square.

Tap the stretcher wedges lightly into position, thus expanding the frame, until the oil painting is stretched taut. There will now be a small amount of canvas overlapping the stretcher frame. Fold this carefully round the corners and tack it to the back.

Stretching a canvas

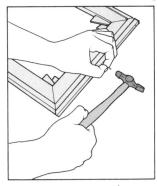

1 Nail batten to stretcher to correct size.

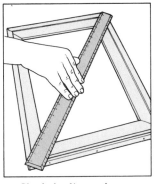

2 Check the diagonals to ensure frame is square.

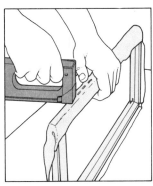

3 Staple canvas to outside of stretcher.

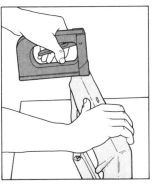

4 Work all round, pulling taut as you go.

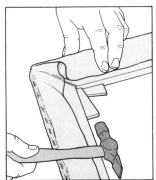

5 Tap wedges lightly into position to expand frame.

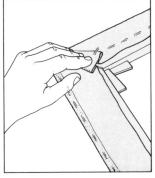

6 Fold excess at corners, and tack to back.

Measuring

Measure the outside of the stretcher frame. Ideally, you should add on about 3mm (⅛in.) to be sure that the canvas drops easily into the finished picture frame. This amount, however, depends on the size of the rebate (rabbet) on the frame you intend to use. Many frame mouldings have a very small rebate; in such cases you will have to allow less tolerance.

Varnishing

Oil paintings, like other forms of artwork, need to be protected from atmospheric impurities. Glass is a suitable covering for many items, but is not recommended for oils. Oil paintings need to 'breathe'; if they cannot, mildew and fungi can become a greater problem than cigarette smoke, open fires, and so on. Varnish protects the oil paint used in the painting and can even be replaced when it deteriorates with age. If you are framing or re-framing an old oil painting, on which the varnish has deteriorated, either take it to a professional picture restorer for re-varnishing, or consult a suitable book on the subject.

If the canvas is not already varnished, it will be necessary to apply a light coat of good-quality picture varnish. There are several suitable products on the market. The paint must be completely hard – a process which usually takes up to two years – before any varnish is applied, so that there is no danger of this becoming mixed with the paint.

Cutting the frame

As we have seen (pp. 34-5), it is possible to cut a frame using a mitre block and saw. For the inexperienced, however, this can be difficult with frames which are more than 25mm (1in.) wide. If your frame is wider than this, follow the instructions closely and take the greatest possible care.

There are two alternatives. The first, if you intend to do a lot of framing, is to consider buying a more sophisticated mitre and saw. Otherwise, get the mouldings pre-cut by a local picture framing shop. It is essential that the cuts are made to true 45° angles – with the type of frames used on oil paintings mistakes can be costly.

Above: *A good-quality picture varnish can be easily applied using a soft natural hair brush, or a wad of cottonwool.*

Below: *There are many excellent mitre saws on the market, but unless a lot of frames are going to be cut, it is difficult to justify the cost of specialist equipment.*

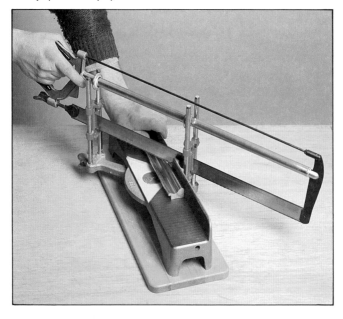

Joining the frame

The most proven method of joining a frame is to use a good-quality glue and nails (see pp. 36-7). This is essential on smaller frames where the area of the mitred joints is considerably smaller than on larger frames, and the weight of the glass and the contents of the frame proportionally greater.

With a larger frame as here, with no glass and just a lightweight oil canvas to be framed, gluing alone is sufficient. Take the four cut pieces, spread a good-quality wood glue on to the mitres, then place the pieces on a flat surface and assemble the frame. Tie a piece of string loosely around the outside edge of the frame, then place two small wooden blocks on each side between the string and the frame. Move these blocks towards the corners and you will find the string tightens automatically. Remove any excess glue with a cloth before it sets, then leave the frame until the glue has set. A good sturdy frame should be the result.

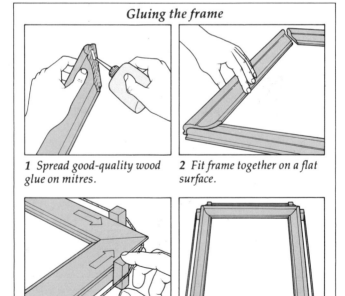

Gluing the frame

1 *Spread good-quality wood glue on mitres.*

2 *Fit frame together on a flat surface.*

3 *Tie string around frame; wedge in blocks.*

4 *Wipe off excess glue, and move blocks to tighten.*

Assembling the painting

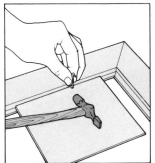 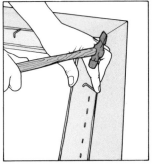

1 *The best method of fixing is to use 'Z' clips between stretcher and frame.*

2 *If these are unavailable, use panel pins instead. Drive into stretcher, then into frame.*

Assembly of oil painting

'Z' clips are used to keep the painting in the frame. To ensure that you do not damage the rebate, place a piece of card (cardboard) over the rebate so that the 'Z' clip is in fact hammered on the top of the card. Hammer one end of the clips into the rebate, insert the painting, then hammer the opposite end of the 'Z' clip lightly into the back of the stretcher frame.

If you cannot obtain 'Z' clips, you can use panel pins which are driven through the stretcher from the back so that they come out of the sides. The stretcher is then placed in the frame and the panel pins are driven further home into the actual frame moulding, taking care not to drive them too far as they will then protrude through the front of the frame.

Project 5: Tapestry

Tapestry kits are now readily available and becoming increasingly popular; many people like to buy these and create their own designs by weaving the wool through holes into the pre-coloured canvas supplied. Apart from tapestries, embroideries, *petits points* and even printed linens, such as tea towels, can all be framed in the same way. The most difficult of these items to frame, however, is a wool woven tapestry created on canvas. Even though these are usually woven with the canvas on a stretcher frame, they tend to be asymmmetrical when they are finished, and have to be stretched square prior to framing.

The tapestry illustrated here will be framed and mounted (matted) in the manner described for the water-colour on pp. 28-39. It would be possible, however, to attach it directly to the frame, as the oil canvas on pp. 40-7 was worked. The way to do this is described on p. 54. If you do frame your tapestry in this way, bear in mind that it will not be protected from the atmosphere, as it would if it were under glass, which is therefore always recommended although some people find it detracts from the appearance.

Left and above: *Mounting and framing tapestries under glass will preserve them undamaged for future generations.*

Stretching

Buy a piece of hardboard (masonite) large enough to allow a 150mm (6in.) border around the work to be stretched. Place a piece of lining paper, or preferably a piece of thin Conservation (museum) paper (see p. 73) on the rough side of the hardboard, then place the tapestry on top of the lining paper.

Starting at the top left-hand corner of the work, fire a staple through the cloth and into the hardboard. Pull the top right-hand corner of the work straight and fix staples all along the top edge of the tapestry. Now, manoeuvre the bottom left-hand corner square and fire another staple through the cloth and into the hardboard. Repeat this procedure in the bottom right-hand corner of the work, making sure that the whole is now square. Pull the bottom horizontal and the left and right verticals straight and staple through the canvas border around the outside of the tapestry approximately 25mm (1in.) clear of the design.

Continue inserting staples all the way round, then turn the board over and flatten the protruding staples using the head of a hammer.

Measuring

Measure the completed stretched work on the hardboard for a mount exactly as described on pp. 30-1. For a tapestry, the overmount (mat) should overlap the work by approximately 3mm (⅛in.); if you were framing an embroidery, for example, you would leave a good border around the work to highlight it. The size of the border depends on how you placed the staples, generally about 50-60mm (2-2½in.) should be sufficient.

Cut the mount card and window as described on pp. 30-3 and fit it over the work. Line it up correctly, then pencil round the outside of the mount, remove the mount and cut the hardboard to the pencilled marks. Trim off any excess canvas.

Take the overall measurement of the piece, and buy a piece of glass to this size.

Usually, a heavier type of frame will set off a tapestry to its best advantage. Read the advice given on p. 44, then either buy ready-cut moulding, or cut your own (see p. 34). On heavier frames, gluing only is sufficient (see p. 46), but if you are in any doubt, glue and nail as described on pp. 36-7.

Stretching and measuring

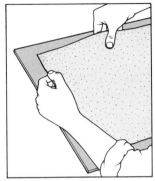

1 *Lay protective card under work.*

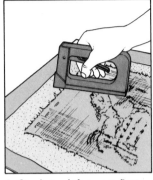

2 *Staple top left corner first, then work round.*

3 *Turn work over and flatten staples.*

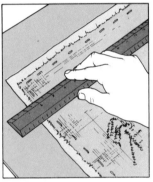

4 *Measure for frame; allow 50-60mm (2-2½in.) border.*

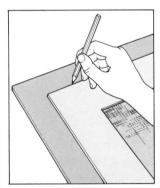

5 *Pencil round outside of mount on to hardboard.*

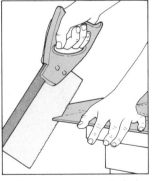

6 *Trim off excess hardboard with a saw or craft knife.*

Assembly

The pieces should be assembled as described on pp. 38-9, although here the backing board and the tapestry are one and the same. After you have cleaned the glass and placed it in the frame, lightly brush the tapestry to remove all dust and fluff, and snip off any loose threads. Brush any dust from the glass, place the window mount in the frame face down and lay the tapestry on top. Fix the tapestry in the frame using small panel pins.

Turn the frame over and check that it has been assembled correctly, and that no pieces of dust have suddenly appeared. If everything is to your satisfaction, you should now seal the back.

Because the back of the hardboard has been perforated by staples, it is necessary to put two layers of tape over both the join and the staples. If you use gummed paper tape, ensure that the first layer is dry before you fix the second.

Assembling the tapestry

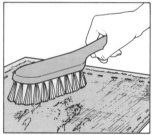

1 Brush any dust from glass and tapestry.

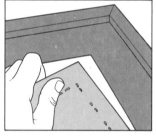

2 Lay mount and tapestry into frame.

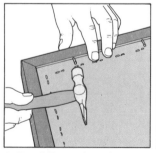

3 Carefully tap in nails to hold all in place.

4 Tape over joints and staples to finish back.

Many works of historical interest have been woven and then framed. Careful framing of tapestries today will preserve them for the future.

Framing fabric items

A well finished tapestry, embroidery, *petit point* or even just a printed linen tea towel can be framed to make it a very attractive and decorative item to hang on the wall. Often it has taken a great deal of time and careful application to produce the finished item, and therefore as much care should be taken in the stretching and framing of these subjects as with any oil painting.

Cross-stitch embroideries are suitable subjects for framing, and can be approached in the same way as a tapestry. If a mount is used take extra care where you place the staples. They should be as far away from the image as possible because the more space left around the outside of the subject, the more appealing is the effect.

Pieces of lace can be framed in a similar way to a tapestry, but, since they have no excess borders around them, they are impossible to stretch. In this case, lay the lace directly on to the mount card (mat board) and frame it as described on pp. 28-39 for a water-colour. A few small stitches will fix the subject to the mount card.

Tapestries which are framed as an oil painting would be, must be stretched over a piece of hardboard (in place of the stretcher frame), then laced tight at the back of the hardboard to pull the image square. This, however, is a time-consuming and laborious process. The alternative is to glue the tapestry to the hardboard using a rubber-based glue of the type usually sold as fabric or carpet adhesive.

Mounting lace

1 *Place lace on top of mount card.*

2 *A few small stitches will hold it in place.*

Stretching tapestries over hardboard

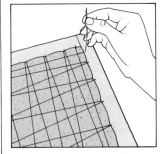

1 Lacing is easier to adjust, but time-consuming.

2 Rubber-based glue gives a satisfactory result.

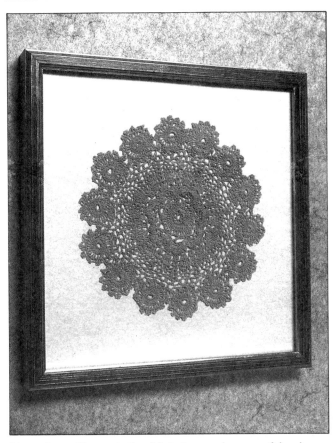

Many pieces of lace and other fabric items make successful and attractive framed presentations.

Project 6: Dried flowers

Framing three-dimensional items

Framing need not be confined to 'flat' images: many commonplace three-dimensional items also benefit from a protective glass covering, and can be framed to create a pleasing and interesting ornament. The most effective way of dealing with such items is, in effect, to double frame them. An inner frame is placed over the piece, and the whole is then framed as usual. In this way, the glass does not touch the item at all. (The technique is similar to using a mount/mat to raise the glass from the surface of, say, a piece of artwork.) Many items make suitable subjects for framing in this way.

As we have seen (pp. 48-55), many tapestries and embroideries can be framed as water-colours; if the embroidery is raised from the surface of the backing, however, or has very heavily textured stitches, it is best treated in this way. Similarly, such items as bead, fabric or shell collages are all suitable for this type of framing.

Small sculptures of stone, minerals or wood can also be treated in this way, and make effective presentations, as do cameos. Similarly, pressed or dried flowers, and grasses, are also successful.

Dried flowers are not usually very deep, so this project is fairly simple. The most important part of the project is ensuring that the inner frame is sufficiently deep so that the glass does not touch the flowers. With a little application, however, the process can be adapted and used with deeper subjects, such as posies, or even bouquets, of flowers.

Due to atmospheric impurities many works that should be displayed openly need to be protected by glass. This necessitates a deep frame, usually made up of two or more frame mouldings.

Preparing the backing board

Dried flowers should be laid on a backing board so that they are displayed to their best advantage, possibly with a few dried leaves to create an attractive arrangement. An ideal background is an appropriately coloured piece of silk, or other material. Velvet or felt is normally used when framing medals, for example.

Determine the size of the arrangement, and cut a piece of hardboard large enough to allow for a generous border around the outside of the flowers. Buy a piece of silk large enough to cover the board, with an allowance for turning down over the back of the board and gluing down. Take great care to keep the threads of the silk as square as possible. Glue the top edge down first with an appropriate multi-purpose glue, then pull the bottom edge and the two sides tight and glue them. Hold the material in place with clothes pegs (pins) while the glue dries.

Arranging the flowers

Now, arrange the dried flowers in the centre of the board. Take the time to get a pleasing arrangement. Most items can be glued to the backing board, but use the minimum amount of adhesive to prevent the glue discolouring the backing fabric. It is sometimes advisable to 'wire' subjects through the backing board – fuse wire is suitable for this.

Leave the arrangement until the glue is completely dry, and the flowers secure.

Inner frame

One of the most appropriate inner frames for this type of work is commonly known as a 'box' (shadow) frame, which has a flat back and sloping inner edges. These can be obtained with edges of varying depths; obviously you must buy a frame with sufficient depth for the subject being framed.

You must also bear in mind when choosing that the top of the inner frame must be narrow enough to be covered by the rebate (rabbet) of the outer frame.

This frame holds the backing board, so use that to obtain the necessary measurements. Assemble the frame as described on pp. 36-7.

Measure the outside of the inner frame to obtain the measurements for the outer frame. Place the inner frame to one side to allow the joins to dry thoroughly.

Arranging the flowers

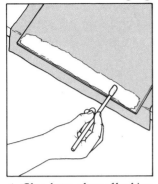

1 Glue down edges of backing material.

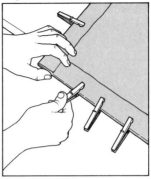

2 Allow to dry; support with clothes pegs.

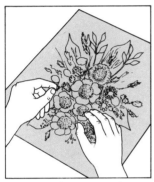

3 Arrange flowers on the backing board.

4 Glue or wire flower arrangement in place.

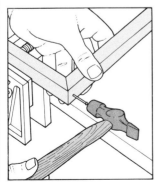

5 Glue and nail inner frame. Measure for outer frame.

6 Assemble inner frame into outer frame with glass.

Outer frame

There are two types of outer frame. One is commonly known in the UK as a 'hockey stick' frame, and is thin and deep enough to cover the depth of the inner frame; the other is wide and flat. If you choose the latter, it must be wide enough to render the sides and fixings of the inner frame invisible to the casual glance, when the finished work is hanging on the wall.

Cut the outer frame to fit snugly over the inner frame and buy a piece of glass to fit neatly over the top of the inner frame, and snugly into the rebate of the outer frame.

Ordinary watercolour type frames are suitable for inner frames.

Outer frames must have a deep rebate to hold inner frame and glass in place.

Joining the frames

Clean the glass thoroughly as described on p. 18. Lay the outer frame face down on a soft work surface and place the glass in the rebate, then drop the inner frame gently into place.

If you have bought the 'hockey stick' type of outer frame, the edges of the frame will protrude above the inner frame. The two frames can be joined together by lightly tapping panel pins into the inside of the outer frame. Take care when you do this: it is important that the panel pins do not protrude over the rebate of the inner frame.

If the outer frame is of the wide flat variety, the inner frame will protrude above the rebate of the outer frame. To keep the inner frame snugly held in the outer frame, tack panel pins into the outside of the inner frame so that they are flush with the base of the outer frame. These panel pins can then be stapled firmly down into the outer frame.

Assembly

Remove any dust from the surface of the glass (use a vacuum cleaner as the glass is deeply inset). Check that there are no foreign bodies or specks of dust in the flower arrangement, and brush any particles from the fabric backing using a soft bristle brush. Set the backing board complete with flowers very gently in the back of the frames.

Although you could use panel pins to fix the board firmly in place, tacking them in might possibly dislodge the flowers. It is better, therefore, to use carpet tape, or a similar strong adhesive tape, to keep the backing board in place.

Finishing

The back of the inner frame can be neatly finished by cutting a piece of brown paper 13mm (½in.) smaller than the backing board and pasting it to it. Gummed paper tape should then be applied to the edges to seal the back of the whole assembly.

Many people find this type of presentation is more successful if the finished article hangs flush to the wall. Two mirror plates should therefore be screwed to the sides of the frame.

Assembling the frames

1 Brush dust from flowers, drop into place.

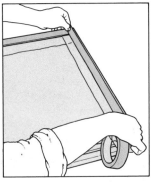

2 Use strong tape to keep backing board in place.

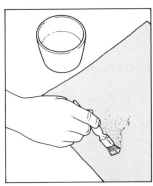

3 Paste a sheet of brown paper 13mm (½ in.) smaller than backing board to back of whole assembly.

4 Seal edges with gummed paper tape.

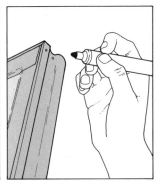

5 Touch up panel pins with felt-tip pen.

Further ideas

Introduction

The experience you have gained and the techniques mastered from tackling some, or all of the projects in this book should stand you in good stead for attempting some of the more unusual framing ideas which follow.

In the last project (pp. 56-63), we looked at framing items other than pieces of artwork. Many items can be mounted and framed, and in this section we look at how to tackle more unusual items, including coins and notice boards.

Card mounts (mats), as we have seen (pp. 28-33), enhance many presentations, particularly water-colours, pastels and prints, but many other types of artwork benefit from an attractive mount. In this section, too, we look at ways to decorate a mount. This decoration can range from a simple ink line, to a combination of lines and wash, perhaps with the addition of gold, silver or coloured tapes. We also consider how to cut circular and oval windows for mounts. This is not an easy technique, but can be successful if care is taken.

Left: *Simple lines on mounts give a more professional appearance, while an attractive frame enhances an ordinary mirror. Medals* (above) *can also be mounted and framed successfully.*

Decoration of mounts (mats)

Artistic decoration of the mount for water-colours and prints can make a great deal of difference to the effectiveness of the display of the subject. To do this successfully, however, great care must be taken; unnecessary or poorly executed decoration of the mount defeats the object of the exercise.

Mounts can be decorated in a number of ways from a simple gold line to a combination of lines with a water-colour wash in between them. Practise repeatedly on scrap board before you start on a real mount. First, decide how many lines would enhance the presentation. Sometimes one line would suffice, here there will be six lines, with some gold tape and a wash in between.

Rule out your chosen pattern on a spare piece of card (cardboard). If you then place a 45° set square against these lines and pencil through them, you can measure along this 45° line to ascertain the distance between the various lines in your pattern. Place the ready-cut mount on the work surface and draw a line at 45° away from each

Decorating a mount 1

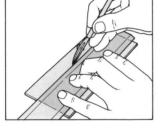

1 Mark out design on scrap card.

2 Scribe through design at a 45° angle.

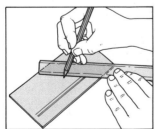

3 Measure distances on line for reference.

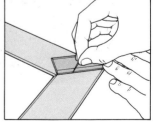

4 Transfer to corner of mount, mark distances with a pin.

corner of the window of the mount. Then, measuring from the corner to the outside, place a pin prick along the line at each measurement corresponding with the trial sample. Repeat this at all the remaining corners, then lightly erase the original pencilled mark. The pin pricks can now be joined up around the outside of the mount.

It is best to use a ruling pen, which can be adjusted to various thicknesses, and good-quality inks or a thick solution of water-colour to draw the lines. Start with the inner line and use an inverted ruler to avoid any smudging. Make sure the first set of lines is dry, before you join up the next set of pin pricks. Gold tape or any other coloured tape of a suitable width can be laid in between two of the inner lines, and a wash can then be applied between the wider of the other two lines.

It is difficult to apply washes correctly as they are basically almost all water with only the smallest amount of colour mixed in. Start at one corner and work in both directions one after another so that the wash does not dry from the point of commencement until completion; this is to avoid tide marks and requires swift application.

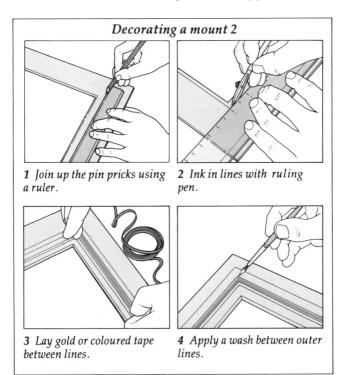

Decorating a mount 2

1 *Join up the pin pricks using a ruler.*

2 *Ink in lines with ruling pen.*

3 *Lay gold or coloured tape between lines.*

4 *Apply a wash between outer lines.*

Notice boards

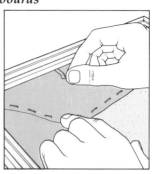

1 *Aluminium frames are effective for notice boards.*

2 *Use springs to hold board inside frame.*

Notice boards

These are easy to make from insulation (insulating) board, covered with felt or with cork tiles and then framed in the normal way, using a moulding which is fairly robust and has a deep rebate (rabbet).

A good method of fixing the felt to the insulation board is to use double-sided carpet tape at approximately 75mm (3in.) intervals and to fold the surplus felt over the edges of the board and staple it down. Cover the whole of the back with a piece of hardboard to hide the ragged edges of the felt and give extra firmness to the insulation board.

Coins

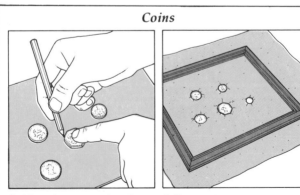

1 *Use coins as template for holes.*

2 *Press coins into coloured felt, then frame.*

Coins

Coins look at their best when displayed upon a felt background. Place the coins on a piece of thick mount card (mat board) and pencil around them, then cut the circles out of the mount card so that each coin fits into a hole. Place a piece of felt over the mount card and press the coins into the relevant indentations. Make up and attach the frame as described on pp. 34-7.

So that it is possible to remove the mounted coins and polish them from time to time, the backing should be fixed with turnkeys (swing clips). These are small arms which are screwed into the outside of the frame and can be turned to release the contents. They are commonly used on ready-made photograph frames.

Mirrors

As mirrors tend to be quite heavy, you must take great care when you join the frame. It is advisable to drive nails into the joints of the frame in both directions for extra strength. To avoid reflections from the rebate of the frame, it should be stained black and the mirror should be inserted into the frame and lined with a soft material such as cardboard behind the mirror to avoid scratching the silvering. Build the cardboard up slightly higher than the depth of the rebate and cut a piece of hardboard to cover the whole of the back of the frame so that the hardboard both keeps the mirror in the frame and also strengthens the frame itself.

Mirrors

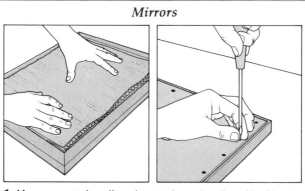

1 Use corrugated cardboard to keep mirror in place.

2 Screw hardboard backing to the frame.

Rather than buying round or oval frames, just as good an effect can be obtained by using a circular or oval mount in a square frame. Good-quality round or oval frames are very expensive.

Oval and circular mounts

Oval and circular mounts used in rectangular frames create a pleasing effect. Oval mounts are particularly effective in enhancing a portrait and are frequently used for miniature portraits. Circular mounts are suitable for many types of small picture, such as birds, butterflies and so on.

It is very difficult to cut small oval or circular mounts accurately by hand, these always look better when machine cut. Unfortunately these machines are very expensive. The cheapest hand operated type, which is only of limited use, costs about £40 ($60). A good machine costs upwards of £200 ($300). Even busy professional picture framers often find it difficult to justify the costs of purchasing such a machine as the percentage of oval and circular mounts used is small.

The following methods of hand cutting can produce satisfactory results provided the mount required is not too small – inaccuracies are more noticeable in small mounts.

Circular mounts are cut with a craft knife. First, using a hacksaw, cut a slot in a Perspex (plexiglas) ruler approximately 13mm (½in.) from one end and at 60° to the horizontal. The slot must be wide enough to accept the blade of the craft knife. Starting about 50mm (2in.) away from the slot, drill holes large enough to accept a panel pin along the centre of the ruler, about 6mm ($\frac{1}{4}$in.) apart.

Place a piece of scrap card on the chipboard work surface, with the mount card on top. Insert a panel pin through the hole in the ruler which corresponds to the centre of the mount card, then put the blade of the craft knife into the slot in the ruler and make the cut. The 60° angle of the slot will result in a bevelled edge being cut. Ideally the angle of the bevel should be 45°, but it is very difficult to do this (it is easy to make a vertical cut, but the task becomes more difficult as the angle from the vertical increases).

Oval mounts are much more difficult to prepare than circular mounts, and must be cut freehand with a craft knife. First, draw the oval pattern; this is done by using two nails and a piece of string. There is no simple formula to determine the length of the string or the distance between the two nails – it is a matter of trial and error.

Cutting a circular mount

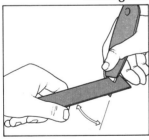

1 Cut a slot in a perspex ruler at 60°.

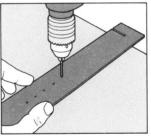

2 Drill holes large enough to take a small nail.

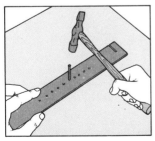

3 Pivot ruler on nail on a new cutting board.

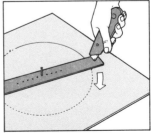

4 Cut firmly with craft knife in one continuous movement.

Lay a piece of paper on the workbench and draw a rectangle which will contain the required oval, that is, the top and bottom and the two sides of the oval will touch the sides of the rectangle. Draw a centre line lengthwise down the rectangle, and insert a nail approximately one-third in from each end of the centre line. Take a piece of string, loop it round the two nails and knot it so that the top of the loop just reaches the top of the rectangle. Put a pencil in the string loop, and mark the paper by moving the pencil as far outwards as the string will allow. The line you draw will be oval shaped and should just touch all four sides of the rectangle. If it does not, adjust the distance between the nails and/or the length of the string. When you have drawn an oval of the correct size, remove the paper, substitute the mount card and draw the oval on it.

The hole you have marked must be cut out freehand. Hold the knife as if you were using a bread knife to cut a loaf; rest the middle joint of your forefinger just outside the line of the oval, dig in the blade on the outer edge of

Cutting an oval mount

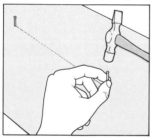

1 *Mark extremities of oval; place two nails on centre line.*

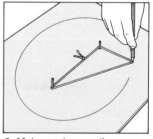

2 *Using string, scribe out an oval.*

3 *Firmly cut round the line – this is the difficult part.*

4 *Sand any irregularities with glasspaper.*

the line and make the cut. You will find that you are automatically holding the blade at a 60° angle. When the cut is finished, smooth the bevelled edge with a piece of fine glasspaper to remove any irregularities.

Conservation (museum) and acid-free mounts for water-colours and prints

Many water-colours and prints are rare or valuable and must be protected from deterioration. Although some of the materials used are impure and prone to accelerate the deterioration of the paper used by the artist, it must be said that the majority of damage is caused by direct sunlight falling on the picture, or by improper storage. Another major factor is staining caused by dampness and impurities seeping through poor-quality or imperfectly sealed backing boards, and thus allowing mildew or fungi to develop.

To prevent these problems, it would be wise to take appropriate precautions when you are working with a particularly treasured item.

The artwork itself must not be allowed to come into contact with any damaging materials. The mount board must, therefore, be of a high-quality acid-free construction (this is a board which has a neutral acidity value of 6.5 pH), and when the painting or print is fixed to the mount board, it must be with the minimum amount of contact as tape is liable to cause damage to the paper itself. Two small pieces of water-soluble gummed paper tape at each top corner will be sufficient, although, if possible, you should use special acid-free tape. The back of the picture or print should then be backed with a sheet of acid-free lining paper before the hardboard is finally put in place.

To achieve a perfect seal of the picture in the frame in order to prevent bugs and mites entering, it is first necessary to seal the glass. This is done by taping the outside edge of the glass to the inside of the rebate, taking care that the tape cannot be seen from the front of the picture. Then, assemble the picture in the normal way and carefully seal between the backing and the back of the frame as described on p. 39. If in doubt, seek advice from a professional picture framer.

Finally, it should be stated that the materials described above are considerably more expensive than those normally used.

Hanging

Many a good picture has been ruined by falling off the wall. It is, obviously, important that the fixing is sufficiently strong to carry the weight of the picture. Any picture of great weight should be hung on a picture hanger which has been screwed into the wall. Larger hanging hooks already have a screw hole for this purpose. For even larger pictures separate fixings should be used on either side of the picture.

Mirror plates, rather than 'D' rings and screw eyes, can be used to hang mirrors flush on the wall, although if

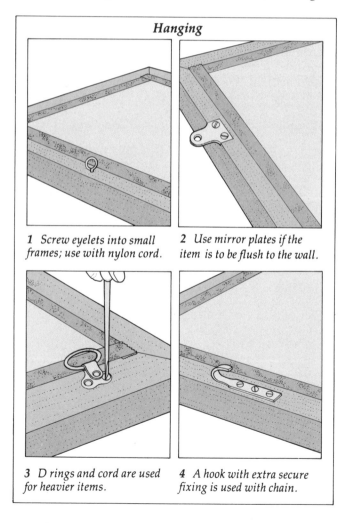

Hanging

1 Screw eyelets into small frames; use with nylon cord.

2 Use mirror plates if the item is to be flush to the wall.

3 D rings and cord are used for heavier items.

4 A hook with extra secure fixing is used with chain.

the mirror is very heavy it is more convenient to use multi-holed plate rings and chain (obtainable from DIY/hardware shops).

If you are hanging a large mirror, attach a batten to the wall for the bottom of the mirror to rest upon, thus supporting its weight. Alternatively, the mirror could rest on a mantelpiece. Use mirror plates at the top and at both sides to attach it to the wall.

The cord you use should be of braided nylon. If you use wire, it is essential to use purpose-made picture hanging wire of the correct calibre. For really heavy subjects, you should use chain.

Hanging mirrors and large paintings

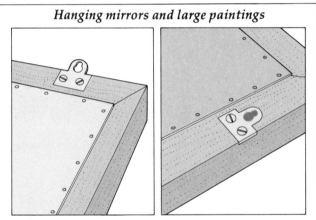

1 *Screw mirror plates to the top or sides of the frame, depending on the piece.*

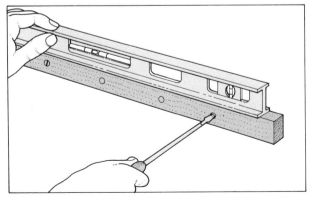

2 *Very heavy items should sit on a batten screwed securely to the wall.*

Acknowledgements

Swallow Books gratefully acknowledge the assistance given to them in the production of *Picture Framing Techniques* by the following people and organizations. We apologize to anyone we may have omitted to mention.

Photographs: Jon Bouchier 8, 9, 11, 12, 16, 19, 20, 24, 25, 27, 28, 33, 35, 40, 41, 45, 48, 49, 54, 56, 57, 60, 61, 64, 65, 70; Elizabeth Whiting & Associates 4, 6, 7, 53.

Illustrations: Steve Cross 15, 17, 18, 23, 26, 30, 32, 34, 37, 39, 43, 46, 47, 51, 52, 55, 59, 63, 66, 67, 68, 69, 71, 72, 74, 75.

Tools on pages 8 and 9 supplied by E.Amette and Co Ltd.

Materials supplied by Mascot Studios, Byfleet.

Poster on page 20 supplied by Frame Express.